ENTERING THE MARE

Katie Donovan was born in 1962, and spent her early youth on a farm in Co. Wexford. She studied at Trinity College Dublin and at the University of California at Berkeley, and spent a year teaching English in Hungary. She now lives in Dublin where she works as a journalist with the *Irish Times*. She has published two collections, *Watermelon Man* (1993) and *Entering the Mare* (1997), both from Bloodaxe.

She is the author of *Irish Women Writers: Marginalised by Whom?* (Raven Arts Press, 1988), and has co-edited two anthologies: *Ireland's Women: Writings Past and Present* (with A. Norman Jeffares and Brendan Kennelly), published by Kyle Cathie (Britain), by Gill & Macmillan (Ireland) in 1994, and by Norton & Norton (USA) in 1996; and *Dublines* (with Brendan Kennelly), published by Bloodaxe in 1996

KATIE DONOVAN

Entering the Mare

To Anne -
thanks for coming
+ many fond
wishes
from
Katie Donovan

BLOODAXE BOOKS

ISBN: 1 85224 429 1

First published 1997 by
Bloodaxe Books Ltd,
P.O. Box 1SN,
Newcastle upon Tyne NE99 1SN.

Bloodaxe Books Ltd acknowledges
the financial assistance of Northern Arts.

Cover printing by J. Thomson Colour Printers Ltd, Glasgow.

Printed in Great Britain by
Cromwell Press Ltd, Broughton Gifford, Melksham, Wiltshire.

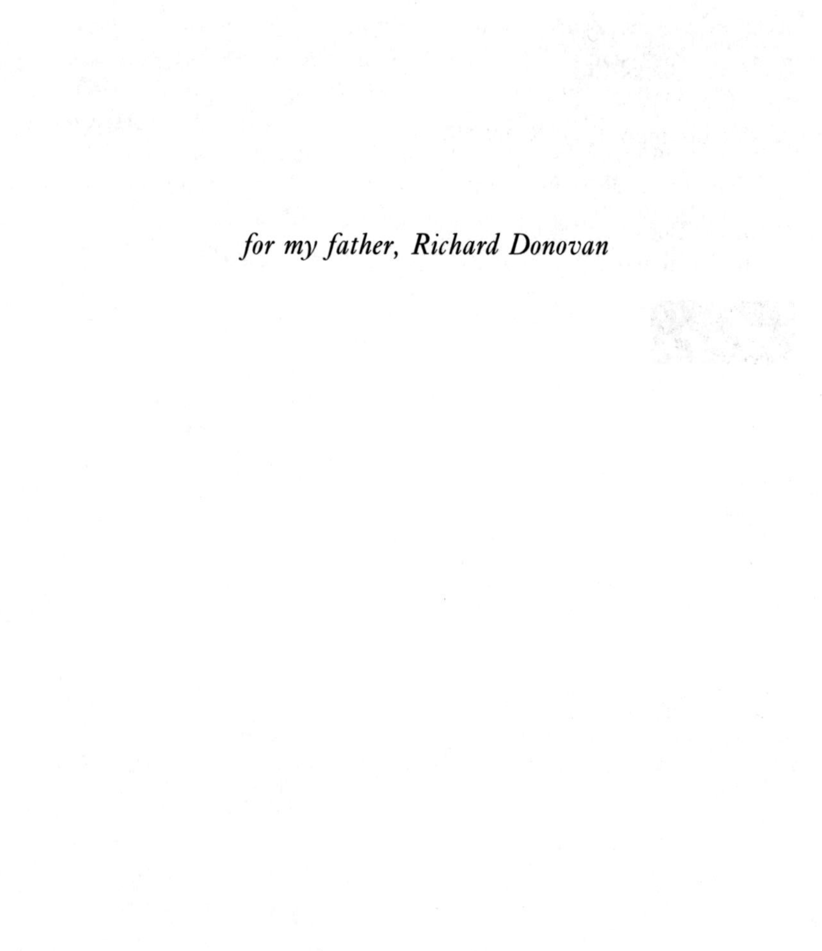

for my father, Richard Donovan

Acknowledgements

Acknowledgements are due to the editors of the following publications in which some of these poems first appeared: *Acorn*, *Force 10*, *Fortnight*, *Poetry Ireland Review*, *Southern Review* (USA) and *Tandem*.

'Totem' was written at the Hay-on-Wye Literature Festival poets' squantum in 1994, and was broadcast on BBC Radio 3.

Thanks are also due to the Arts Council of Ireland and the Irish Writers' Centre for sending me on a Writer's Exchange to Paris in 1995, where I worked on some of these poems.

Contents

HUNGER

Strike

I will sit outside your door,
my body shrivelling.
Not a taste of food
will I put through my lips,
just the odd swallow of water
to keep my tongue in working order
should anyone pass and look,
and wish to know your fault.
Think of me as you sit inside
at your full table,
a glass of stout
and a plate of hot food before you.
I am starving
that the world will know your cruelty.
I sit here so they will see my wasting:
the dimming of my eye,
the closing of my ears.
As I fade, your injustice
begins to fall away
from my brittle back
like a rough cloak
I need no longer carry.
I am moving beyond pain.
But my story thrives
even when I can no longer tell it.
It lives in the mouths
of those who have heard and seen me.
They are going to give me
the biggest wake
the town has ever known.
They will gather at your door
and take my vigil.
But they will not starve.
They will feed on my blood,
my bones, the last morsels of my sweet flesh.
They will swell with my outrage.

Make no mistake:
they are waiting for you.

Hunger at Doolough

The black lake is full of skeletons,
from the hundreds who trod the famine walk,
knocked on the door of the big house,
and were turned away.

On their long trudge home,
the lake wind took them
in bone-flinging gusts,
tossing thin, weary limbs
into the water,
where they swallowed death.

Luncheon was still being served
in the big house;
the lake – a pool of dark calm –
was shimmering through
the tall windows.
The governors of the town
lapped it with their soup.

We drink it now:
the lake, the long green sides
of the valley, the flinty rock
and curling mists.
We drive the quiet road,
and fill up on tranquillity;
we bloat with the view,
thanking our luck
we are the only ones here,
and have it for ourselves.

A few old farmers
leave their raddled ewes
to waddle the slopes;
they have said their piece
to TV microphones:
'You can't eat scenery.'

That is why
they'll sell their stony stretch
to fill their bellies,
on the week-end spree
of a lifetime.

They'll feed
the hungry claw
of the strip-mining company,
come to scratch
for gold.

Gold and bones
are hidden
in the valley
of the black lake;

and even as we turn our faces
to a rare caress of sun,
we are not satisfied
by the panoramic meal,
rolling out its solitary hauteur:
the falls
is a thrust of white water
at our thirsty eyes,
the wild pink rhododendrons
and yellow flags
lure our appetite
with their clever garnishing,

but biting in and quaffing down,
we find only a bitter taste
of greed.

Out of Her Clay

Out of her clay
comes rose,
cabbage,
tree,
stone.

Her largesse
is boundless,
and because
it is given
into my hand,
into my mouth,
I must deserve it;
just as the sea
laps me,
salves my child's wounds,
washes my lungs
in her fine breezes.

How easily we become orphan.
In the hunger time
the earth bred only rot:
her gift was a stinking grave.
The fish in the sea
swam free, mocking the shore,
where men lay
in wasting weakness,
their boats long sold
for bread.

All the years since
of full bellies
have not fed us.
We are orphan in our hearts,
and how we punish her
for her abandonment.

We use her open arms
for dumps and factories,
we pour our poisons
into her spawning beds,
we foul the sea.

How long will it take
before her inevitable
spitting back:
toxic waste,
plastic bags,
supermarket trolleys,
seething towards us
in a vast black claw:
psycho mother wave.

Neck

Between the wig
and the blue satin dress:
her neck.

She is borne in a tumbril:
the crowd licks its lips,
thinking of the blade.
She has been dreaming
of blood falling
in a warm stream
down her breasts;
now she feels the breeze
at the small hairs
of her nape.
She feels the slime
of spittle
on her lowered brow;
hears curses rise
in a clot
around her.
She looks up once:
the women's eyes
are hating hard,
the men's cheeks
are reddening
with drink and rage.

I will give my head
for my father's big house;
for my education;
for the unusual dishes
we ate at table.
I will give my head
to them
who had nothing;
who starved;
who crawled with vermin;
who stank of poverty.

She remembers
her parents' feuds
and lovers;
the painted parties;
her favourite horse.
She remembers running hungry
through large, dishevelled rooms,
afraid, her small feet
cold on the marble tiles,
her belly crying
for bread
in the lonely dawn,
her voice trained
into silence
as the mansion slept.

They will carry my head
in a basket
and set it upon a spike.
All night
they will tear
each other's clothes
in fear or lust,
and my head
will watch,
the blood
cooling
and congealing
on my white
neck

City of Bread
(Paris, November, 1995)

I followed a trail
in the city of bread
on a fresh Sunday:
people walking home
clutching baguettes,
red-nosed in the winter air,
ready to enjoy a feast.
I found the open stalls:
trays of oysters, shelves of camembert,
the boulangerie crammed with croissants,
decked with long loaves,
hot and fragrant.

This is the bread of life:
the journey to find and eat,
the air keen on the cheek,
the mouthful of bread
satisfies the morning.

In this city of bread,
they gave their blood
to feed me from a full oven.
They knew there is no sure thing,
except a fistful of bread
snug in the palm.
Without bread you are without sense
or saving, heads must roll,
and swords must pierce the heart,
until the nose is calmed
by the smell of a crust rising.

Life is held in the warm
crunch and flake
and melt of good bread,
rolled on the tongue,
the comfort in the swallow.

My life is bread.

New York City, 1947

You were ten years old,
on your first journey
to the gleaming fruit,
that was ripe
for eating then.

It was all excitement,
party shoes,
and you on your daddy's arm.
You were his princess,
for a few precious days,
staying at the Plaza,
breakfasting
with him alone,
before his business meetings.

It was Broadway lights,
Central Park
covered in Christmas snow,
shopping and malted shakes:
all those frostings
on the cake of childhood,
that you hoarded and inflated
in the dreary adult winters
of rural Ireland:
no central heating,
no maple syrup,
no movies;
just up at 6 o'clock,
to milk the cow
and churn the butter.

You offered me your icons
as a dream of childhood
I could never have,
so when I made my way
to the big apple,
I thrilled and shivered
on the huge, dirty streets,

I passed up and down
like a hypnotised tramp,
before the massive facade,
and immaculate doorman
of the Plaza.

It was my afternoon off,
and soon I'd be back
in the Brooklyn flat,
where no air conditioning
cut the humid meltdown;
where I was nanny, maid,
consumer of leftovers:

nibbling
at the still bright crumbs
of your childhood's
New York.

Journey

We travelled far,
moving into the landscape
of burnt yellow flatlands,
distant blue-headed hills,
dark spindles of trees,
branches reaching
for the fragment of rainbow's arch,
which hovered, faded,
reappearing always
further off.
Our road dipped to scoop
the metallic lap of floodwater,
covering the hollows in boggy fields
like quicksilver,
swans beaking their plumage
in white, looping movements,
feathering the marshy grasses.
Mountains mint green in sun,
patched with shelving red bracken,
shifting in rain shadow.

We strayed, looking,
cheekbones chilled in wet winds,
our insides churning
with the urge for movement,
as streams burst down and down,
boiling away rock, moss, old wood.
We dallied by a graveyard,
you lost in camera angles,
while I walked away
suddenly a stranger.

Our noses brought us finally
to the road for home,
we ate again the miles
of discarded searching –
the dregs of our journey –
digesting painfully
the return.

Shepherd Boy, Transylvania

(for Attila)

He fingers the stiff keys
of the old church organ,
making the music
of his life on the mountain:
the wind heaving
past his narrow hut,
the yawnwhine and bark
of the shaggy dogs,
the bells jigging
on the jostling throats
of his sheep.

His green eyes
shine through dusty air,
as he fills the space
with sound,
like a bucket
fills with milk.
He is gaining the top of the mountain,
the animals running before him,
the dogs urging,
his own steps quick and sure.

But then his playing falters,
like his bad leg
on rough ground.
His new friends herd him
out of the church,
and on to the next adventure
of this strange day together,
a day that has him scrubbed,
put in his best clothes
and driven to odd places.

His friends
stuff sweets in his pockets,
block the sting of the wind

with a bright blue anorak,
give his poor feet pride
in white hightopped sneakers.

They want more:
to take him from the rough rhythm
of his old life,
from the acrid mouth
of his father,
from the smell of wet wool
on his hands.

They will not hear
his wish to stay
for the black-toothed song
his wages give the old man,
for the clean silence
of the mountain air.

Their questions confuse him,
he would rather listen
to the tinkle of the girl's breast
when the wind pulls the silver ball
around her neck. He shuffles,
his eyes travelling groundwards
at her nearness.

Fingers descending to the wet grass
he pulls out a ripe windfall.
Leaning to gather the firm, fragrant shapes
in his chapped hands,
he finds at last a return
for his friends' impossible gifts.

His smile bursts when they stand silent
to chew his apples,
and he knows
the swollen wealth of giving,
and why
they have come to him.

Yearn On

I want you to feel
the unbearable lack of me.
I want your skin
to yearn for the soft lure of mine;
I want those hints of red
on your canvas
to deepen in passion for me:
carmine, burgundy.
I want you to keep
stubbing your toe
on the memory of me;
I want your head to be dizzy
and your stomach in a spin;
I want you to hear my voice
in your ear, to touch your face
imagining it is my hand.
I want your body to shiver and quiver
at the mere idea of mine.
I want you to feel as though
life after me is dull, and pointless,
and very, very aggravating;
that with me you were lifted
on a current you waited all your life to find,
and had despaired of finding,
as though you were wading
through a soggy swill of inanity and ugliness
every minute we are apart.
I want you to drive yourself crazy
with the fantasy of me,
and how we will meet again, against all odds,
and there will be tears and flowers,
and the vast relief of not I,
but us.
I am haunting your dreams,
conducting these fevers
from a distance,
a distance that leaves me weeping,
and storming,
and bereft.

Sweet Woman

He'll go
after he has dug
a big space out for himself.
But first, he likes
a bit of resistance:
it's a challenge.

When, eventually,
I cave in,
he tramples around
my heart, lungs, lights,
until he has
a good comfortable bed
made
in me.
Then he leaves.

Then I'm a leaking wreck,
ready to double over;
the wind rattles my guts.
That's when I curl around
the empty space,
that's when I nurse
the hollow.
I rock the hungry voice;
I feed her,
I sweeten her loss,
I block her crevices
with happy tastes.

When he comes back
I'm a round display
of treat-me-nice
sweetmeats;
there isn't a niche
in the packed shelves
of my ribs
for him to get
a toe back in.

Warm Hand, Cold Heart

I reached in
to the glowing spread
of your sun-tongued flesh,
to find your heart.
My fingers coaxed the door,
it opened slowly,
snagged in rinds of frost;
the white heart breath
streamed forth, to offer me
cold cuts, snowed in fruits,
all the fare you'd buried
in that frozen core.
Out came:
your mother's dish of bile;
the clotted cries you swallowed
as your father beat you down;
the waif wings
of the girls you loved,
because they made you strong;
the party dishes
your jaded palate left aside;
the arctic lens
of your hermit's
watchfulness.

Your warm hand
laid a table
of aromatic meat,
and good wine;
but your heart
fed me on hoarfrost,
the pitted shrink
of rime;

and now
the door is closed,
and I am left
with a bellyfull
of ice.

Flush

Lost in the trees,
she's away from the white lure
to empty herself out.
She is rapt
in the simplicity
of wood and water;
the campfire flames
offer hot, charred food:
she swallows easily
its burnt gold glow,
squatting, hands out in the dark,
thinking of the deer
foraging beyond
the fire's ring.

Back to weekday
city pretty lights,
billboards, heels,
the mirror's leer,
and the white voice
comes calling.
One tile follows another,
to the porcelain cavern,
with its jaw spread wide.
She is heaved beyond her will,
flushing like a well-behaved girl,
to leave no trace
of what her gut kicked up;
crying deep
in the red cavern within,
for something more and less
than pizza and ice-cream.
She dreams of chopping logs,
and the clear force
of the river:
she would drink deep
to spit
that aftertaste
of acid.

Making Shapes

What you need
is whalebone,
underwire,
and padding
to lift, squeeze,
and magnify:
to give you a shape.

We all know
there's no hope,
unless a man can feel
like he's holding
two ripe melons
in his hands,
or else be fooled
into the promise
of heavy fruit,
cleft, and up
for grabs.

The ideal choice
is the remould:
slash and stitch,
a bag of jaunty silicone
on either side,
and next year,
you'll be Mrs Right.

The year after that
you'll have scar tissue,
a burst balloon
inside you,
your glands marching
against the foreign matter,
your brain on fire –

and everyone telling you,
you knew
what you were doing.

Sick

Your face blurts red,
your stomach rises,
you crouch
and hang your head
over the foul gut-lurch.
Wasted, your eyes swivel
up the street,
your lips gummed with shame.
Your first concern,
is to sweep away the mess,
you fuss
with cleaning,
bending over your belly,
wondering when
you can change your dress.
You stagger with the passing
of the spasm, patting
the hiccuping spawnchild within.

Do you think
the drunken men
of the town
care one whit
for clean pavements,
as they slide open their flies
and thrust out their waste?
Do you think they care,
as they heave into the gutter
dollops of their night's excess,
before running off
for a refill?

But you, who bursts with life,
must clean yourself away,
hiding from the voices
of your own,
who will judge you,
as surely
as they forgive their men.

Lockjaw

They gave you the wrong pills again,
and now your jaw is locked open.

This is how your body
tells the story of your life:
whenever someone
filled you with careless poison,
your mouth opened to protest,
but no sound ever stepped
into articulation of outrage.
Instead there was a bitter swallow,
while the others plucked the fruit,
complaining about the worms they found,
their blistered hands.

You were left unfed,
the honey in your arms for sharing
was taken, and your blue-eyed,
freckled smile was smudged
by the clumsy swipes of those around you:
the graspers, the talkers,
the demands of the discontented.

Even when your nourishment
is piped through a mean tube,
still they come
to baffle you with pettiness.

But now, with your staring eyes
and open jaw,
you are a mask
of paralysed disbelief,
so terrifying to behold,
that all who see
the locked jaw
fall silent,
their words
evaporate.

They leave you
to fight the enemy inside alone,
frozen by the wrong drugs,
your face staring,
struck in a pose
of weary surprise,
that your body has borne
all this,
and is somehow
still alive.

Report

'Celibacy is the greatest pain of my vocation.'

The words come cleanly
from your kind, thin-lipped mouth.
I take notes,
feeling my skin heat,
avoiding your eyes.
This is only a morning in my routine,
but with your wide palms
you hold your whole life out to me,
to be shaped by the whim
of my angle.
Your face contracts
in memory of the search
that led you here;
while all I can think of
is your body,
meant for nakedness,
sitting across from me
in a white robe and a black hood.
A junior brother,
you are the youngest
among the grey-haired,
and I am the first woman
to explore the cloister.
My pen slides in my grip
as I walk the corridors,
thinking of your bed
which has known only
prayers and pain.
Coming here
to 'escape the emptiness
of worldly things,'
you found a greater hunger.
Now you hope for God
'in the afterlife',
and today
the sanctuary splinters
as our hands touch.

The Man With No Child

He dreams
of planting his seed,
and pulling out
the wet plum
of the new life,
when time comes ready
for harvest.
He feels the years
gathering in him,
crowding his heart,
thinning his bones.
He is father in every sense,
except that for which
his globes of genesis
were formed.
He nourishes the stripling,
the stray,
the chance unhappy stranger,
the disconsolate friend,
the neighbour's sick child,
the burdened and tainted earth.
He feels as though
he is the father
of his own parents.
They do not dissuade him.

As the seasons taunt him
with their busy parade
of regeneration;
he settles into solitude,
like an ageing tree
beside a holy well,
branches laden
with the pennants
of hope and expectation,
hung there by pilgrims
who have come to drink
the waters of the well.

They depart light, carefree;
he remains,
garlanded with their leavings,
father of their abandoned dreams,
supporting
what they could not carry.

In spring
he still feels
a vein rush:
tormented, he waits
by the secret mirror of the well,
and all that he can see
is the reflection
of his own thirst.

Spits

Small boys appear
in shiny, lollipop suits,
crew cuts and freckles.

They are too young
to be disarmed by womanhood –
I'm just another moving target
for the hail of blind words,
which land like poisoned spits
in the quiet waters
of my inner ear.

With sure-flared nostrils,
they are drawn
to the victim in my eyes.
They pull my bag,
grab the keys,
hijack my car,
and demand
a chauffered joyride.

Their hoarse shouts
explode the kind angel in my head.
I want to kill them.
I want to break their little legs
like wizened sticks,
and roast
their marble-sized testicles
on a spit.

But nobody can catch them,
even if they haven't got
a matted pony to lash
into the sunset.
They are a school
unto themselves, small fry,
swimming through the meshes
of the nets
that trawl for larger prey.

Their shoal operates as one,
the snatched bag
travels effortlessly
from hand to hand;
the car window
shatters
like broken teardrops,
on a medley
of tiny, kicking feet.

Gambler

Smoothing his black hair,
his loose legs thrown out,
he is dishevelled,
the way ash caves
around a central glow.
Out of his huge green eyes
tongues a reviving flame,
as he remembers living high,
when he took the four grand
his aunt gave him,
handed over half
to stall the courts
on his unpaid mortgage,
and stuffed the rest
in his underpants.
He lost it in a night.
The spill of fear,
then the cool column
of certainty,
growing in his spine;
the swagger, the fall,
the black pit –
then the redemption
of the new bet.

Now he keeps a job,
a wife and children.
His dark skin no longer beats
with the bloodsurges of chance.
Now he crushes the lustre
of a new success story,
before its dazzle
consumes his reason.

His extravagant eyelashes
sink with their heavy lids,
but behind the screen,
the green eyes
are blazing still.

Choosing Fiddles

(for Brendan Mulkere)

His chin leans down
to her gleaming hip,
his fingers settle
on her slim throat,
he smiles
into sounding her,
his fond eyes
resting
on her well-formed curves.

He has already tried –
and left aside –
the one with the short neck,
the one with the showy voice,
the one that would not sing.

Now he draws
the searing lilt and call
of her, the bronze delight
of polished wood;
the ready strings
beneath his stroke
and swoop
become a loosened flight
of feathered notes,

falling
pure and long,
turning back again
for the release
of his big,
searching hands.

Muse

I need his blood
to comfort me
in the slow fail
towards winter.

I need his breath
to blow life
into my sap,
set me readying
with buds
and pushing leaves.

My palate craves him.
Let him be brought
to my chamber.
Let him be strong
and succulent,
as he enters me,
torching his light
into my darkness.

Buried there,
he'll work
his long spell
until I throw up my hair –
scattering the stars.

I will find
the lost music
of my throat
in the piping
of his melodies.

I will peel back
my dying skin,
build again
my young face
out of his tender rivers,
his perfect bone.

TOTEM

Entering the Mare*

She stamps and shivers,
her white coat vainly shrugging,
as the would-be chieftain
plunges in, burying deep
his puny, acrid man's seed,
between her fragrant haunches.

The Goddess lives
in her fine rearing head,
the pink stretch of her lips,
the wide, white-haired nostrils.
Her hoof
might have crippled him,
her tail
whipped out his arrogant eyes.
Instead she jerks clumsily,
trying to escape
the smell of his hand.

Later he swims
in the soup of her flesh,
sucking on her bones,
chewing the delicate morsels
of her hewn body.

He has entered the Goddess,
slain and swallowed her,
and now bathes in her waters –
a greedy, hairy, foetus.

Rising from her remains
in a surge of steam –
her stolen momentum –
he feels a singing
gallop through his veins:
a whinnying, mane-flung grace
rippling down his spine.

Riding off on the wings
of the divine Epona,
he lets loose his dogs
to growl over her skeletal remnants,
the bloody pickings
in the bottom of his ceremonial bath.

* *The inauguration of an Irish chieftain, as observed by Geraldus Cambrensis (Gerald of Wales) in the 12th century.*

Macha's Curse

She knew why
he did it:
he was a small man
with nothing
to speak of,
so to give himself
a leg up,
he boasted
about her;
how she could beat
all comers
with her fleetness,
faster than any horse
in the royal stable.

After he gave away her scent,
the noses came sniffing
at her hem,
and the king decreed
she show her colours,
or show the world
her husband was a fool.

She was carrying his name –
the name of a simpleton
she rued the choosing of –
in her puffed out belly.
But the king would not wait
even for another month,
when she'd be lean again.

She went alone
to the track.
She saw her husband,
watching,
among the men
to whom he'd spilled
her secret.

She set her teeth,
knowing that the race
was all about
his reputation:
he had put his pride
like a crouching,
sharp-kneed rider
on her back,
urging her to win
for his sake,
even as she ached
with the tiny spurs,
pressing her
from within.

She took her place
between the horses,
a small woman
in a plain dress,
dodging the hooves
and jostling haunches.

The whip cracked:
her bones leapt.
Her jutting belly,
and bloated ankles,
her tired spine –
all disappeared
in the might of her stride.

She shook her dark hair,
opened wide her breath
in the sweet pounding
of the track;
she smelled the sweat
of the horses
as she passed them by,
it sang in her nostrils
of long fields
starred with clover,
of vaulted hedges
full of birds,
and tails frisking in the dusk.

And then it was all
behind her:
the mayhem
of the crowd,
the panting foam
on the horses' lips,
the dim world
of her husband's house.

She fell
on the finishing line,
and in a giant shiver
her body opened
to pour out
her twin young,
their damp new heads
flushed red
with the speed
of their mother's gait.

She lay, empty,
sticky in her blood;
the men
were quieting the horses,
the women
were tearing strips of cloth
to wrap her babies in.

She took the lifestore
of her placenta
and put it
between her teeth,
swallowing back something
of all she'd given.

A great curse
began to gather
out of the ravage
of her torn flesh,
and she let it grow
until her voice
was strong enough
to make it heard:

'I curse all you men
who forced me
out upon the track,
knowing my time
was near,
just wanting
to see me bested.
You'll never have
the winning strength
I had today.

'Whenever strangers come
to fight you
for your land,
you'll find yourselves
cast down by the pangs
of a woman
in her labour,
and then you'll know
what your bets and boasts
have done to me this day.'

Lasting nine days
and passing down
nine generations,
the curse came on them:
whenever they had most need
of strength,
they found themselves
laid low
by Macha's word,
all their gallop stopped
in the heave
of her scarred birthing.

She wrung them out
like dripping shirts,
and hung them up
to dry in flitters
on the cutting line
of her cantering curse.

Horse Sense

It took the Lord
six days
to make the world,
and it takes a mare
six days
to consider,
to shy,
to startle,
flirt and nibble;
to canter,
trot and gallop,
circle and snort,
to lift her tail
and lower her head,
to begin to savour
his scent
in her nostrils,
to feel alright
about rolling
in the dust
with crazy hooves
in front of him,
to bite
his velvet flank,
cast her eye
several times
over his fine head
and girth,
kick up her fetlocks
and let him chase.

But there's no time now
left for any lingering
over the act of creation.

She is led out and hobbled,
back legs spread wide,
a strange stallion
kicking, rearing
and starved
is set on her,
to rend her
like a hot poker,
in front of
the sniggering yard men.

It would never
be like this
if she had her way;

if she were free,
like the wild horses
in the mountains,
she would take six days
to organise her miracle,
following the Lord's example –

or maybe
he followed hers.

Workhorse

Red gums
of your frothing mouth,
lips peeled,
head thrown,
caught
in the tripwire
of battle.

In Vienna
you prance
like trained poodles
to a gallery
of clicking tourists;
butcher shops
sell equine steaks
on Paris streets:

workhorse
you tread a girdle
round my gullet;
mouth chafed,
your satin coat
greasy with sweat.

Stumbling in circles,
you have forgotten
the way out;
all you can think of
is how to keep on
carrying the load.

Slip the panniers,
shake off
the blinkers,
rear and arc
over the wall
to freedom.

You'll grow
a fairy bone
from your forehead,
and in your lightened shoulders
feel a tickling:
the beginning
of wings.

Dressed to Kill

(after St George and the Dragon by Paolo Uccello)

He straps himself
into his metal suit,
and sharpens his weapon:
to win the princess
he must kill the dragon.

The dragon's lewd breath
will burn up
all the good
in the princess,
there will be nothing left
of her candyfloss gown
and red Smartie smile,
the white marshmallow
of her skin
will go black
in the dragon's fire.

He will slay the beast
and wed the princess,
a guileless girl,
without the horns and wings
and devouring fangs he fears.

He wants her grateful smile,
her gossamer body
swooning in his arms,
the slain dragon
beneath his mail-shod heel,
the kingdom
within his grasp.

If he lets the dragon live
she'll crack him open
like a walnut,
pry him out of his shell
with one curious claw;

she'll toast his skin
with her throaty flame,
bite off his head
and gobble it down.

Dressed to kill
he's ready to do battle,
but here comes his prize
leading the dragon
on a golden chain,
she warns him
even as he points his lance
at the snarling jaw,
she will not have him
if he harms the creature;

he must take her,
dragon and all,
her long white neck
and the scaly bulk
of the reptile's gizzard,
her mild front
and the dragon's smoky leer:

he must put down
his blade,
or go home
without his crown.

A Vision of Hell

The Bosnian woman
who is able to touch Our Lady
smiles her shy half moon of teeth:
she has seen heaven,
where happy souls
drift together in long robes.
She visited Purgatory with Our Lady:
it was like a fog,
with lost souls calling –
beseeching her to pray for them.
'But hell,'
presses the chat show host,
'Tell us what hell is like.'
The woman inclines
the pale bud of her head.
She has seen hell,
thanks to Our Lady.
She has seen a beautiful girl
who had negative thoughts
consumed by flame
and transformed into a beast.
The woman's eyes
are bright chestnuts;
the studio audience
applauds.

My cat stirs,
throbbing her pleasure song.
I stroke her thick fur
which thrusts
its innocence
between my fingers.
I would visit
that visionary's pit of doom,
endure the flame willingly,
to emerge as natural
and pure as this beast,
stretching her belly
for love.

She Whale

Great creature
carrying her calf upon her back,
strands of mermaid hair
about her stupendous head,
what has she to fear
from tiny men?
If they fall from their vessel
she bears them up
to air, gently,
like her own young.
They are no bigger
than the flip of her tail,
and their language
is equally minute
in stature or range.
They have no song like hers
to saturate their element
with sophisticated sound.

Imagine her surprise
when a crowd of such herrings
in a floating box
shoots a harpoon
into her head:
the shock of the grenade,
the explosion of the thick darts
that pierce her inside out.
Death comes in
through tent-like lungs,
collapsing them at last,
sucking in water to end,
like a struck man would,
by drowning.
Her tail is lashed
to the ship – a trophy –
her body leaking blood,
and her calf is left,
rending the waves
with its terrible cries.

Display

In the centre of the page,
let's put a large photo
of the winning artist:
his long hair blown back,
his lips reaching to kiss
the woman he has dressed
in a fetching suit
of polka dot, to match
one of his huge tableaux.

Let's talk about his art,
how he cuts up dead cows
and puts their bodies
in formaldehyde, displaying
the severed parts
for our delectation.

Meanwhile, let's give
a small paragraph, no photo,
to the news that the earth's caul –
which allows us to breathe
without frying –
is now torn so wide
that two Europes could fit
in the rupture.

Perhaps soon
it will be our own burnt
and disfigured limbs,
that will float in the ether
of the stratosphere,
for the delectation
of flying saucers
and their wide-eyed passengers.

Cervical Cut

I

Legs yawn apart
in the chemical-scented,
black and white tiled room.

This is where the cutting
is done, so quick
you'd hardly know it.

The metal grips
of the new,
state-of-the-art machine
sink in deep.
The needle numbs,
and the abnormal piece
of pulsing pink,
is severed
like a cankered bud.

Body jolts queasily
back to solid ground,
groin swaddled,
a throbbing gape
within.

II

Night is frenzied
with dreams
of a trapeze lady
hanging from a pendulum.
Inside her spangled pelvis
a monster is growing.
Helpless, she watches
as her soft flesh is parted,
and a scaly, metallic tail
grows out
between her plump, dangling,
dancer's legs

Changeling

'Are you Bridget Cleary, my wife, in the name of God?'
MICHAEL CLEARY, Tipperary, 1895

Another woman
grows inside me:
she curls her lip,
she talks back.
She uses my voice
for taunting,
to try and open his eye:
to see what's wrong.

He says I'm away
with the fairies,
he tells the neighbours
and they agree.
They sit in my kitchen,
goggle-eyed, waiting
for signs.
She won't give them
the satisfaction,
she says:
'Yes, Michael, I am away,
to the place
your mother used to go.'

I know, even as
I hear her say it,
I've pushed him too far,
lifted the skirt
on the thing
I'm not to name.
I'm weak enough –
though I'm wearing
my Sunday best,
never wanting them
to pity me –

I haven't much fight,
for all my rising words,
so when he flings me down
I can hardly say
my name, a lapse
that gives him the rope
to hang me;
the proof he needs
to show them
I'm a changeling.

That's when the fire
burns my face,
and they all watch him,
and I know I'm gone
and she's gone,
the woman
who came and did this
with my voice,
she's left me
a shell
to be torched,
my flesh crackling
in front
of my own hearth;

and him saying always
that I was gone,
I was away
with the fairies,
and putting
the hot flower
of the log
to my brow,
and all our neighbours
watching.

Magic Brushes

(for Phoebe Donovan)

I

Brooms and butterchurns,
aprons and tongs,
pitchforks and bonnets:
scrubbing brushes
and feather dusters
body forth
'spectral evidence'
used to blacken bones.

Martha Cory made mysterious ointments,
Sarah Dashton was a haggard burden,
Anne Hibbens displayed turbulent passions,
Elizabeth How practised the healing arts,
Mary Johnson was discontented with her chores,
Elizabeth Knapp had an apparent teat
in her private parts,
Elizabeth Proctor did the Devil's work,
Mary Sanford planned
to make merry on Christmas.

Iron shafts
stab through muslin nightgowns;
a broomstick
becomes a cross.

II

My great aunt,
had you lived
in the fantastic strait jacket
of that time,
you would have followed
the line to the flames.

I see you, dressed
in your stained painter's coat
and felt hat,
dragged before the bailiffs,
stripped to find the witch's mark,
your body shared around
like spoiled meat,
your house and garden
taken for the godfearing.

Instead,
your brush-strewn studio remains,
with its paints and potion bottles,
charms of driftwood and dried flowers,
canvases of copper brambles,
cow parsley and crab apples,
charcoal men in shirtsleeves
at the threshing.

I enter and breathe in
the evidence of magic,
astride the broomstick
of your memory.

Tenterhooks

(for the Wynne sisters, who ran Avoca Handweavers, c. 1927-1967)

My maiden cousins
were wearing thin,
like old, light-leached cloth,
when my child's footsteps
first approached
their shadowy house.
Blind Winnie
stooping over the tiny faces
of the primulas she bred –
her magenta offspring –
and smiling in the sun.

I loved the leaf and heather
alive in the wool they dyed:
woven and wet
and pegged on tenterhooks,
it was a gorgeous ribbon
down the hill,
for passengers on the Avoca train
to marvel over.

I am certain of a time
when they knew what it was
to be bright and ready,
hung in the heat of an afternoon,
waiting for the right man
to step off the train
and claim his billowing beauty.

But Em's love died in the war,
leaving her with a ring
and a black dress;
Winnie found her bloom
in rich earth,
the touch of petals;
Veronica
stole scraps of time

for her books and easel,
woven in the loom
of her sisters' choices.

The new-dyed cloth
is me now,
throwing out my colours
in the heat:
ochre, madder,
blackberry, fern;
a rainbow
suspended over
the summer grass,
my glory dusted
with the pollen
of hill flowers –
daisy, clover, buttercup –
waiting
in the warm breeze,
for the teazling
of my nap;

until the day's end
when I am rolled
up tight,
cut down to size,
the golden day
a short-lived fragrance
in my muted colours,
my folds dry
and brittling.

That's when I'll slip away,
take my sun-blinded eyes
to my garden,
and breed primulas alone;
my ears deaf
to the sound of trains,
insensible to the tread
of sometime visitors.

Stitching

(for my grandmother, Marjorie Troop)

I send my needle
through ravelled wool,
catching the loose ends
into a cross-hatched darn.
This is how your freckled hands
smoothed the worn spot
over the wooden mushroom.
Pigeon-breasted in your mustard dress,
you bent your head,
snicking in the needle tip,
your fingers light and careful,
as you impressed upon me
the importance
of learning how to sew.
Your favourite backdrop:
a soprano soaring from the gramophone,
the sun sweeping in from the garden,
flouncing yellow swathes over your shoulder.
I have the quilt you made –
my limbs are lapped
in its glowing sunflower heads –
your last opus,
left for your daughter to finish,
and me to admire.

Tomorrow the quilt will be packed away,
part of the unpicking
of the home I stitched together.
I will wander the empty rooms
like you,
when your darning days were done,
and you woke up
in a strange place,
surrounded by strangers,

pulled apart,
the gap too wide
for mending

Grooming

(for my mother)

Dreamy and docile you sit,
as I comb out
the long ends of your hair.
Like mine, it is thin and straight –
a hairdresser's nightmare.

I have played with your hair
since I was scarcely
tall enough
to reach your reclining shoulder.
My small hands,
busy with their child's work,
seemed to comfort you.

Now you sit, slackly,
sighing as I pat and snip;
the brown swatches fall,
veined with grey: a splash
of last year's growing months.
Your face is delicate and girlish
as I guide the angles of your head.
My palms push you into reverie,
my pulls and swipes,
my amateur measurings,
my fussy trim.

It is a clumsy job.
Yet, as always, you shake yourself,
toss out the flattened strands,
and pronounce yourself glad.

Regretfully, you rise,
and go to sweep
the chopped grey-brown fluff
of your shorn locks,
as though cleaning out
the cluttered bedding
of a staled nest.

Totem

(for Catherine Church)

Out of the tide
of generations,
your cheekbones resurface
in my face,
your eyes slant mine
into blue almonds.
I have your Christian name,
and an old photograph
where your sepia mouth
closes in a prim
half-smile, half-rebuke.
Your long hair –
which I fondly think of
as a dark river
down your back –
is pulled tight
with severe Victorian pins,
your high, plain collar
stiffening your chin.
He has a kind face,
the blonde whiskery man
who married you:
your conversion
made you half-respectable,
malleable in your apology
for your savage blood.

Where did the tribal sap go
when you found
the stern father-God
and a white husband?
Did it rage
in your whalebone corset,
kick in your belly
like an overdue birth?

I imagine your torn days
shrugging off the Iroquois fears

of your husband's circle,
setting your face
against the clan mothers
and moon visions;
keeping your eyes fixed
on the stark body
of a milk-limbed man,
hanging from a cross;
your dreams flooding
with the heads of wolves
and beavers, the shiver
of the earth
beneath the thunder lunge
of buffalo.

This was your freedom:
a half-life,
yet perhaps you could see
the dwindling path
of your people,
now leading to a lost reservation
pumped with quick cash,
souvenir shops
with their heart-breaking canvases
of winging birds,
the numb bodies of your men,
out of their heads
with drink,
so that when the white car
runs over their legs,
they don't wake, or feel,
they lie bloating in the ditch
waiting for the end.

Is this what you saw
when you changed your name,
and squeezed
the wide, high arches
of your feet –
which I have inherited –
into shoes which never
fully fit, and will not
fit me now?

Blade

Here is your sword:
you have lain
your body down
upon it,
your head at the hilt,
your heart at the cross,
the blade
is cold beneath your spine.

You offer yourself
as the channel
for your vision
of advance;

I fear you will be
trampled, forgotten,
or found by your father
and impaled.

Stoic

I push my face down,
forcing my body
through the cold water,
that presses and chills
my fugitive breath;

I wait until
my head
is a trapped icicle,
and my lungs
are lined with frost,
before rising
to my native element.

I open my numb lips,
take one long, fabulous
suck of air,
feel the warm hands
of the sun
on my face;

quickly then,
before the pain
of thaw,
I'm back under,
braced for the current,
the cuffs of waves,
the frozen, salty sac
of this mother
who tries to force
me out,
but I'll not quit:

while there's strength
left in me,
I'll hold my breath,
and struggle on.

Stone Journey

(Winter Solstice, Newgrange, 1995)

Seeking a warm entry of light
I went to the mound,
pushed through the tight stone passage
to the centre.

Chilled
in the memory of bones,
I waited for a golden shaft
to bless the chamber,
to coax the stone spirals
into catherine wheels of glory.

I waited
for the flooding of the cavity
with the promise
of summer fruiting,

but the dark was broken only
by a trickle of grey,
creeping in
from a morning laced with rain.

The gap was filled
by a woman's voice,
crying against the huge capstone,
for a broken harvest,
a lost child.

The Big Woman

(for Geraldine)

A piece of the sky
fell on her head,
and all the rivers
of the earth
poured out of her eyes:
the Big Woman was dead.

She woke
in the cold darkness,
thinking the longest night
would never end;
but then the horizon beckoned,
in a slow wave
of apricot bubbles.

She leapt from her bed
and into the dawn:
all her limbs and belly,
and magnificent head;
the sun was her skin
stretching in a rosy flow,
across my window.

'Come and be
the Big Woman,'
she called,
as the wind played
in her chestnut hair,
her eyes alight
with the warrior gleam
of maternity.

I watched her,
and my heart was tight:
'I am not big enough,
nor woman enough,
to follow.'

She laughed,
her bright teeth
flirting with the rim of the world.
She said she would swallow me,
just as one day,
when the Big Woman died,
she was swallowed,
all unknowing;
and one day,
she would die,
and I would take her place.

I couldn't tell her
that the line ends here:
her like
will never come
again.

The Face, the Situation

The face has the dignity of stone:
the head carried just so,
the eyes deep and opaque –
there could be monsters
and mermaids swimming there,
but I will never know.

The eyes do not see me.
I obtrude myself.
There is a faint flush
in the cheek, a bow.
The eyes slide over
and lose me again.
The profile is ancient;
aristocratic. The lips
proud and closed.

Just when I think
I am invisible,
and begin to hunch
and creep, like a worm
beneath the queenly toe,
there is a new situation.
The mask flexes and is gone,
the lips stretch
in a hesitant smile.
The eyes are glad,
they rest on me.
I am weighed on a regal scale:
I tiptoe on my mettle,
I tear into the moment,
I defer, I claim attention,
all on the sudden trusted urges
of an inner rudder:
the arrow of myself
which I must hope is true.

Now I am close to the face
and find it glowing; I nestle,

and wonder at this change.
Then, I remember,
the situation is always
metamorphosing, and the face with it.
Tomorrow I may be
dust again, the face shut
against me like a palace door.

But now a quiet hand
is offered, and the face,
marvellously soft,
offers itself
to be kissed.

Earthed and Airy

You have been too long
inhabiting the sky:
your blood rushing
with the clouds,
your arrow of light
quickening
with the storm clarions,
your eye
beaming on the land,
your wings
sweeping you on.

I found your tail
and pulled you down;
like a wind-weary kite,
your feet were glad
on earth,
your hand
was a shooting star,
falling hot and magical
into mine.

You gave into gravity
to let the heft
of your body
sink into me,
you came down
into the weight of yourself,
and held me
in the delicious press of you,
owning the solid stone
of your name.

I tied my string
around you,
fluffed my feathers
and took to flight,
shook the dust
from my plumage,

sheared away the gathered
moss and mould
of my caved winter,
opened my throat
and sang to the sun.

When you wound me in,
my hair was a mad dance,
my face red,
and my eyes
full of the horizon.
Earthed and airy,
we hid in the long,
marvellous hours,
but now comes

the letting go

Blossom Time

(Tokyo, April 1995)

Crown of blood-orange,
and the sun comes up electric,
shearing off the woolly cloud;

a procession of brides
is floating down the hill,
arms held out,
heads held high
with veils of pale pink,
and trimmings
of wakening birds.

All day the pilgrims gather
to pay homage; all day
the brides pose,
delicate in their finery.
I wander beneath
their rapturous milk rose sprays,
confetti of petal
softening in my hair.

Dusk comes, bruise-coloured,
and the nymphs
take up their night poses
beneath my window,
fists of flowers
holding off the rain.

They pinken my dreams
with cherry lace and sap,
underskirt of leaf;

morning finds my plodding body
fragrant and aflutter,
and I come up molten
with the sun.

The Devil in the House

Floating on wingtips,
I halo the street
with my sugar icing smile;
get me home,
and I'll scorch your hair off
with my devil's breath.

Out of my satin pumps
my hooves clatter up the stairs,
off come the flesh-cramping clothes,
and out pouts my belly,
growling with relief.

How carefully I inspect,
and brush and scour
my poor unready self
to spill like new milk
out into the street
and light up your life,
my cheery white hand extended,
my tireless ability
to lay down my tunic
over your dirty puddles.

Now I'm home,
fangs unleashed,
I'm ready to bite
the hand that feeds me,
grub around in the filth
of my dwelling,
curse the day
I ever had to share this earth
with any living soul:
devil-happy, horny-clawed,
my wings hung up
for the night.

Gobnait's Shrine

The pilgrims are paying rounds
to Gobnait:
their lips
murmur over her grave,
their feet
scuffle past her church.
They bring their hopes to her well,
tie scraps of cloth to her tree,
slide their handkerchiefs
across her mighty bowl.
Standing on her sill,
they reach
to the sheela-na-gig
who dances over Gobnait's window:
pilgrim fingers touch her
with sudden intimacy, bare arms
reaching up through the narrow arch
to caress the stone sheela,
whose happy centre is worn away
with rubbing.

I watch the man's forearm
and reaching hand,
and feel myself
firmly grasped, my own parts
reverentially fondled, praised;
the overture of a dance inside:
Gobnait is whirring in the foxgloves,
the fragrant grasses,
the moving stream.
I drink from her waters,
taste her in my mouth:
her rising white trout;
her nine deer;
her magical bees
– whose avenging stings
drove away cattle thieves –
her agate bowl
that razed the invader's castle;

the sorry head of the man
who stole her horse,
and was hung after.

Gobnait, my heart is toasted
in your kitchen;
in you I find a place
I felt I could not claim,
where I can reach my hand,
dip my cup, hum
my own incantation.

Notes

Strike: The hunger strike is an ancient form of protest in Ireland. In medieval times, it was enshrined in Irish law as a means of demanding redress. The aggrieved individual would sit outside the house of the offender, 'fasting against' him.

Hunger at Doolough: This poem was inspired by the story of six hundred people who died in 1849 (during the Great Famine) at Doolough Valley near Louisburg in Co. Mayo in the manner the poem describes. The area – which is very picturesque – is currently a focus of interest for gold prospectors.

Macha's Curse: Macha is the character in the eighth-century Irish epic, *The Táin*, who puts a curse on the men of Ulster because of the reasons outlined in the poem. A woman with supernatural powers, she is clearly a personification of the horse goddess.

Magic Brushes: This poem was inspired by 'Requiem', an installation by Barbara Broughel, depicting 42 people, mostly women, executed as witches in 17th century America; also by the independent spirit and talent of my great-aunt, the painter Phoebe Donovan.

Cervical Cut: In Ireland alone, an estimated 2000 women have this operation every year, which involves cutting out pre-cancerous cells from the cervix.

Changeling: This poem owes its existence to the research of folklorist Angela Bourke into the burning to death of Bridget Cleary in her own house, by her husband, who apparently believed the fairies had taken his wife and left a changeling in her place.

Stone Journey: The winter solstice is a special occasion at the megalithic mound in Newgrange (constructed *c.* 3500 BC). The mound has been designed with a light box, so that when the sun rises on the morning of December 21, the sun's rays penetrate into the central chamber. This event, with all its symbolism of the sun fertilising the earth, cannot occur however, if there is rain and grey skies.

Gobnait's Shrine: Many fantastic deeds are attributed to St Gobnait, whose shrine is in Ballyvourney, Co. Cork. A sheela-na-gig is a medieval carving of a woman exposing her genitals. They were often carved on churches by superstitious stonemasons who believed that the sheela would ward off evil spirits.